WHISPERS IN THE MEADOW

Lavender Bilbruck Smith

WHISPERS IN THE MEADOW

Vanguard Press

VANGUARD PAPERBACK

© Copyright 2024
Lavender Bilbruck Smith

The right of Lavender Bilbruck Smith to be identified as author of
this work has been asserted by her in accordance with the
Copyright, Designs and Patents Act 1988.

All Rights Reserved

No reproduction, copy or transmission of this publication
may be made without written permission.
No paragraph of this publication may be reproduced,
copied or transmitted save with the written permission of the publisher, or in
accordance with the provisions
of the Copyright Act 1956 (as amended).

Any person who commits any unauthorised act in relation to this publication may be
liable to criminal prosecution and civil claims for damages.

A CIP catalogue record for this title is available from the British Library.

ISBN 978-1-80016-920-3

This is a work of fiction. Names, characters, businesses, places, events and incidents
are either the products of the author's imagination or used in a fictitious manner.
Any resemblance to actual persons, living or dead, or actual events is purely
coincidental.

*Vanguard Press is an imprint of
Pegasus Elliot Mackenzie Publishers Ltd.*
www.pegasuspublishers.com

First Published in 2024

**Vanguard Press
Sheraton House Castle Park
Cambridge England**

Printed & Bound in Great Britain

Dedication

Dedicated to Drew, without whom I would have nothing to write about. I wish you all the happiness and love that this world has to offer. Thank you for the journey, it was a wild one.

Eye of the Storm: Part 1

The eye of the storm never seemed
As calm as your eyes did
After you fell out of love with me
The soft, sea blue eyes
That once held such warmth
Are now as cold as the abyss
It hurts too much to look away
But I am torn asunder
By the sharpness of your gaze
If God were merciful to my plight
He would tear out my eyes
And veil me in darkness

Beauty

"He's beautiful" I thought
As I watched him rejoice over a victory

"He's beautiful" I whispered against his temple
As the morning sun kissed his skin

"He's beautiful" my heart sobbed
As I left his house, all my possessions in my arms

He *is* beautiful.
But his beauty left me broken

The Devil

I looked into his eyes and smiled
Damn
But the Devil is beautiful

Weakness

If he kissed my eyes
And asked me to die
I would impale myself on a sword
As cold as his words

The Sea

His eyes look like the sea on a calm day
Warm, inviting, and promising unbridled joy
The only way I could have prevented falling in love
Would be to never have known him at all

Commitment

I'd follow you down to the pits of hell
And drag your ass up to the sun
But you push me away
With empty words
And take my life
With a heart shaped gun

Numb

Frost bites at my lips as the warmth leaves my body
I sit, eyes unseeing, limbs unfeeling
My heart as still as if I'd died
The only thought on my mind:
How foolish I had been to hope

Mercy

Take my life
I gladly impart every last ounce of my being to you
Keep my sanity in a bottle and throw it into the sea
You have destroyed who I was and who I was to be
Finish what you started
Have mercy
Please

Despair

My eyes burned with fire
As I screamed into the night
Begging
Bargaining
But I was met with suffocating silence

Self-Destruct

If I break my bones on the cold stones of sorrow
And rend the flesh from my body
Could I reform myself
Into something you haven't touched,
Something you could never break?
My skin would be harder than granite
And my heart stronger than ruby
Athena, grant me wisdom
And Tyr, grant me justice
And Lord, grant me mercy
I am on a path of destruction now

Bargaining

If I whisper your name fondly
And battle all of your demons,
If I comfort you when you need it most
And offer you all of my strength,
Will you love me better?

Disappointment

Disappointment stings
It tears at my self-worth
Until all I'm left with are questions of why
Was I not enough to tempt you?
Was I not as beautiful?
Was my love not as pure as you needed?
My world shatters because you pointedly ensured my disillusionment
After all this time I am still weak for you
And the disappointment I feel stings like the venom of a black widow
A treacherous love

The Fool

I squeezed myself dry to fit in with your world
And when you left, I was empty
I had to build myself back up
And I did
But then, once I was whole,
I begged you to come back
I wanted to prove to you
That I was so much more than you ever thought
It was foolish
It was vainglorious
To think that because of my awesome beauty
You would have stayed by my side

The Devourer

Steal my breath, I beg of you
Wrap yourself up in my soul and steal the warmth from my heart
Take all the pain falling from my eyes to quench your thirst
You stole my capacity to love
So please
Take it all

Deleted

Select all, delete
And just like that, I am gone from your life
Like I had never existed
Like we had never made love while drowning in our own laughter
Like weeks prior we hadn't been dizzy with joy
Like you had never stepped into my life and whisked me away like a strong breeze
Like your name never spelled my freedom
There is no undo button
I am gone
And I am alone

Worthless

You threw me away like garbage
And I was left bereft
Drowning in my own inadequacies
When I told you I'd love you forever, I betrayed myself
Because here I am in solitude
Still loving you completely
Was I nothing more than a means to an end?
A hobby to fill your time?
No
Even hobbies are remembered fondly

A Prayer

Dear God
Is it possible to find myself?
I gave away the best parts of me
And now I am in need of something
Anything
To fill the void
I beg of you
If you have any mercy
To spare my pain
At least make me numb
Or forgive me my transgressions
Against my own being,
Or bless me with the ability
To love myself unconditionally.
I want to love myself like I loved him.
I want to see myself as a blessing
Or a miracle,
Or a human worthy of kindness

Driftless

I am lost without your presence
How do I find myself again?
How did I let myself become a shadow of the ferocious beast I once was?
I want that version of me back
I want to return to my awful power
Must I claw my way out of the depths of depression, and scream to the horizon
Pleading for mercy?
I forsook my identity for an ounce of your love
And all I have now is the bitter taste of regret on my tongue

Undignified

Desolate
That's how I must appear
For I have lost my will to go forward
Pathetic
Weak
I have disavowed my dignity
In the pursuit of your love
A fallacy
The greatest regret I have
Was ever saying hello to you

Eruption

Want burns in my chest like magma
Ready to burst from my eyes like the eruption of Vesuvius
Ready to cover my soul in ash
I'm ready to lose myself and become like the legend of Pompeii
Maybe in a thousand years my desire will be uncovered
And these words will paint me immortal
Or maybe I'll be abandoned
Left to obscurity
Is it okay to have lived in pain?
I am burning up with devastation, self-deprecation, and shame
I feel consumed by the heat of it
Crushed by the building pressure
Doomed to watch myself implode
Doomed to live a life marred by a crater in your shape

Precious Gemstones

Tears fall from my eyes like diamonds
Loathsome and hideous diamonds
Their existence bathed in blood
Why couldn't my sorrow be stained
With the deep, passionate red of rubies
Or the soul-swallowing blue of sapphires?
Is my pain so pitiful
As to be overshadowed by the bleakness of diamonds?
Can it not be beautiful?

I cry because I once knew happiness
Happiness the shade of topaz
Shining like the sun
And yet my tears fall down my face
Cutting my cheeks
With an absence of color
And a tainted beauty

The Tower

The hardest pill to swallow
Was realizing you would never
Fight for me the way that I fought for you
So hard was it to ingest
That I choked on it
Tears stinging my eyes
Chest heaving as I gasped for air
None of this would have happened
Had I chewed you up and spit you out
But I always had a habit of biting off
More than I could handle
Pity me
I was such a fool
For so long I choked on your apathy
Throat tightening around it like knives
I remember the pain of it
And the sadness that consumed me

The Bare Minimum Destroys

I fell in love with your potential
That was my first mistake
You had every opportunity to be better
And chose not to
Perhaps I was unfair to obligate you to my expectations
By asking you to love me the way I needed
I set the bar too high for you
You could have jumped into the heavens and still never reach my standards
Maybe you weren't enough
Or more simply
I was too much
In the end, you were the bane of my existence
The harbinger of my anxiety
Peace does not exist within you
And love does not exist within your embrace
That limbo was as exquisite as it was heartrending

Pain

Your eyes are blades
They cut me into a million pieces
Your words run over the wounds
And burn like acid
And while it stutters in your presence
My spirit remains indomitable
Next time
I will face you strong in my will
And untouchable

Recognizing Cycles

I'm a traumatized fool out of love
In love with the idea of love
And unconditionally self-sacrificing
I am strong in my weakness
The want to be cared for
At the expense of my own needs
Toxic love tips the scale in its favor every time
And the hand of fate drags me down
To my own personal hell
Burned by apathy
Begging for a crumb of affection
And lost to my own grief

You Can't Love People into Loving You

For six long years you gave me pain
It accompanied your love
And it embodied your departure
With every lie you killed my heart
Until it became a withered, ugly thing
I became less of myself through you
I should have run that day
When you promised me disappointment
And here we are
At the end
With the only promise you ever kept
And you're a stranger to me now

Maybe

Maybe I'll never get over you
Maybe my body will never forget
And maybe that's okay
Maybe you were a lesson hard-learned about the dangers of falling
    into obsession
Maybe this was always supposed to be my punishment
Or maybe you're just a coward
But maybe I am too

The Aftermath of Obsession

I wasn't able to walk away without you making me leave
I don't see myself anymore when I look in the mirror
I see tiredness
And overwhelming emptiness
And incomparable sadness
It's more than a little exhausting
And less than a little welcome
Maybe in the deep recess of my mind I think
This was my punishment all along
It tears me apart, soul detaching from my mortal flesh
Mourning the living
And living in absence
Death has a welcome embrace for me
But I am damned
If the long-dead fire in my eyes doesn't demand I take responsibility
for my heartbreak
Yes
You ruined me
But maybe I'll be found by a lovely, encouraging, understanding,
Everything-you-couldn't-be kind of person
Or maybe I won't; but I'll rebuild myself, just in case
I'm not so far gone as to commit the crimes against love that you did
All in the name of a broken man

Queen of Broken Hearts

I yearn to be as steadfast and as immovable as the oldest oak in the forest
And I crave the flexibility and impermanence of the summer daisies outside my house
The whisper of your love is like a gentle breeze through my hair
Blowing cold on the tears that stream down my face
Allowing them to fall into the soil, to water the roots of my being
Blessed be the fond memories I have of you
And damned be the lovers who lost themselves to love

Dreams are Sweeter

You were still talking to me in my dreams
So I never wanted to wake up

Broken Promises

I promised I wouldn't fall again
And I stayed true to my word
I jumped
Willingly
Into the slow death of unrequited affection
Friendship is less painful
When I am alone
Your words make me ache
And I realize now
It is better to let you live as I love
Than to die in the bitterness of expectation
You were always meant for better
And I was always meant to run
I'll see you in another life
And maybe then I'll be enough

Gratitude

You ripped out my still-beating heart
And ate it
And all I could do
Was stand there and thank you

Celestial

A supernova pales in comparison to the brightness of the flames I carried for you
At least I have undeniable proof that I am alive
That I had been blessed with love
Or cursed with love
Or cursed to have known you at all
Do you think I betrayed myself to feel these things for you?
Did I betray the love and respect I held for my own person
Just to feel so inadequate in the face of your existence?
You once exploded my vision into a shimmering galaxy
And then left my world as void and as endless as space
Will I ever love myself more than I loved the way you made me feel?
Will I ever look at myself and see what I am without you?
There must be more to the universe than the stars in your eyes when you looked at me
There must be more to me than the emptiness you left in your wake
If I have to search to the ends of every planet in every dimension to find who I am after you
Then I'll start my journey with an apology on my lips, and determination in my step
I am sorry to have wasted love on you
And I am determined to exist in the peace of your absence

Grow

I asked God for a sign
I begged on my knees
Until they were bruised and bloody
I cried, torn apart by desperation
Until rivers ran deep with my tears
I waited, with bated breath
Until every second felt like a knife in my lungs
I had given up on receiving an answer when you came to me
In the moment that hope left me
You validated my pain
Reinforced my journey
And promised me healing
My soul fluttered alive with the grace I had received from you
The space to take the first leap forward
Into the generosity of the world
All pain is temporary
But growth is eternal

Rhetorical Questions for the Void

What does it mean to have loved
And then lost?
Is pain the only thing that the heart beats for?
Does bitterness creep into the depths of it?
How does one cope?
Life has lost its flavor
And all around me, grey seeps into my vision
Perhaps
If I become a fallen tree in the woods
I could forget the happiness that I had
Or perhaps
I am beyond relief
I have loved
But not every love is meant to be

Pity Party

How do I love myself?
How do I show myself care?
I never learned how
Maybe
I'll let the world swallow me whole instead

The Phoenix

Maybe if I cut off all my flaws
And weld on some virtues
I can change myself
I will change myself

I am better than you could
Have ever imagined
The power I have
Over my destiny is unparalleled

God gifted me anger
And I will rage
Until I am satisfied
With the gift I have received

You said "later" when you meant goodbye
And I gave to you my sorrow
Wishes of peace and happiness on my lips
Finality in my actions

Do not contact me again
I cannot bear the disappointment of you

Disgust

You took the coward's way out
And I let you
Thinking your peace was greater than me
Forever I weighed your wants over my needs
Forever I shrunk myself to fit your life
Your betrayal is nothing in the face of my own
But I can't help but place my anger
And disdain at your feet
I wash my hands of you
May you die with a thousand swords in your heart
And the crows feasting on your eyes
May you love
And lose
And know what it means to be broken
I wish all of these things
On a coward with no name and no love in his heart

Rage

Fuck you and your bitch-ass excuses
Fuck you for telling me your ex was better
Fuck you for every time you made me feel like I wasn't good enough
And fuck you for saying I was good enough to fuck, but not good enough to date
And fuck all that ableist bullshit
When I was struggling to survive and you called me lazy
Fuck you all the way to hell and back for blaming me for my trauma responses
The least of what you owe me is leaving

Greyscale

If life was simple
Then you'd be the villain of my story
And maybe I'd be the villain of yours too
But life is seldom simple
And villains rarely exist in true evil
There were good times
Beautifully magnificent times
And then there were the worst heartbreaks of my life
What seemed like endless betrayal at your hands
And yet, I can't help but think
Maybe you felt the same way about me

The Journey

The journey was hard
And it broke me
But each step that I took away from your memory, was a step that I took toward myself
Until I was running into my own arms
Until I made myself cry with the joy of my own presence
I may always carry the scars that you left on my soul
But I am an adventure story, and the next chapter is better
I remember the first breath of air I could take without the weight of you on my chest
I remember the first glimpse I had of myself in the mirror without the stain of your hands on my body
The thoughts of you come less often and with less pain
Instead of agonizing screams
They fall upon my ears and brush over my skin like whispers in a meadow
Do you remember when we sat in the park and talked
And cried
And parts of us died
But then parts of each other grew in the empty places?
I remember walking with you to the store and glancing at your face
And wanting to cry with the joy I felt from your presence
And I remember a time I couldn't breathe without you

Twin Flames

You were the love of my life
But not every love is meant to be
Rest in peace, my heart
You died valiantly

The Bliss of Slumber

I hope you always haunt my dreams, my love
The time has passed for you to linger in my life
But I wish to tell you how I love you still
And how happy I am to have known you at all
And how blessed I was to be your friend
These are the kind of wishes that are best left to my unconscious mind
Where I can keep you close for all time
As I wake, I think back on you fondly
But as the morning sun rises, my hold on your memory lessens
The image of you fades in my mind's eye, and in its place reality appears

Fear of Missing Out

I hold my tongue out of respect for you
And your new life
I bite down on the cursed thing until it bleeds
I swallow up my sorrow and allow silence to prevail
I remind myself to let you go
I have never loved someone more
Than I loved you when you were mine
And I'll never love someone to that degree again
I let my soul break from the pressure once
And while sometimes it may still crack
The fissures threatening my demise
I don't break. I can't. I won't
I reject vulnerability, a recent failing of mine, but
I have found happiness in someone else now
I am loved. I am content.
But while this man is all that I need
I can never love him the way I loved you when you were mine
I'm not strong enough to let go
I'm not brave enough to dive in
I know this man is the perfect one for me
Soothing all my pain
Validating all my fears
But he's not you
And you're not mine
So I bite my tongue
And swallow the bitterness

Forgiveness

He was my other half
And I had to regrow the part of me that died when he left
I had to face the reality that I wouldn't ever be more than my inadequacies to him
I had to learn to forgive myself for loving long past the expiration date of our fling
And I loved you deeply
As deeply and passionately as I love the spring
You were my favorite season
But every season has an end
My only hope is that I can learn to love summer even more

Self-Care

It starts with baby steps
Make sure you're eating
Set a routine
Don't forget to shower
If you can, clean your room
Protect your peace
Distance yourself from those that hinder your growth
Lastly
Find out what you love
Follow your passions to the ends of the earth
Peace comes with growth
Pain is just a page
It's not your story

Self-Acceptance

I bathe myself in mediocrity
And I find no fault in that
For I exist as I am
And even though flawed, I am art

Strength

Strength becomes me
I sat on the battlefield
And fought hand, tooth, and nail
I laid down my life for love
And lost what I'd known myself to be
In the end
I emerged with strength
Beyond what I could understand
Strength becomes me
I will wield it like a weapon
Until I slay my own dragons
Princes be damned

In Spite of

I would kiss the dew off my own lips
I would fall into bliss with myself
I would pluck out the stars from heaven to adorn my ears with
Given the chance to love myself the way I loved you
I would worship the ground that I walk on
And then, it would be for someone who deserves it

Eye of the Storm: Part 2

The eye of the storm never seemed as calm
As it did when I first really saw myself
When I looked into the mirror and
Gazed at my battle-scarred beauty
I realized then how breathtaking I was
And I'd fight to the death to prove it
My strength I wrap around my shoulders like a cloak
Confidence and grace are my weapons
And self-love is my shield
Do not doubt me
For that would be your greatest mistake

About The Author

Author of *Whispers in the Meadow*, Lavender Bilbruck Smith is a traumatized, mentally-ill, thrill-seeking goblin. They thrive on helping friends, family, and acquaintances "live la vida loca", and often times runs themselves ragged trying to experience everything the world has to offer. Never one to shy away from adventure, Lavender has dedicated their life to embracing the Chaotic Energies of the Universe and being their true, authentic self. Their hobbies include hiking, rollerblading, daydreaming about being a fantasy warrior, listening to power metal, and watching science fiction B movies. Whispers in the Meadow is their first poetry collection that was written in the throes of heartbreak. It chronicles the messy transition from pain to anger to acceptance. They hope that in putting this collection out there others who are going or have gone through a similar pain can find solidarity and validation within these words.

www.ingramcontent.com/pod-product-compliance
Lightning Source LLC
LaVergne TN
LVHW041547060526
838200LV00037B/1172